T0144316

Spring in
New Hampshire
and Other Poems

Spring in New Hampshire and Other Poems

Claude McKay

MINT EDITIONS

Spring in New Hampshire and Other Poems was first published in 1920.

This edition published by Mint Editions 2021.

ISBN 9781513299907 | E-ISBN 9781513223506

Published by Mint Editions®

MINT
EDITIONS
MintEditionBooks.com

Publishing Director: Jennifer Newens
Design & Production: Rachel Lopez Metzger
Project Manager: Micaela Clark
Typesetting: Westchester Publishing Services

Contents

PREFACE

The writer of these verses was born in the Clarendon Hills of Jamaica in 1889. In 1911 he published a small volume in the Negro dialect, and later left for the United States where he worked in various occupations and took courses in Agriculture and English at the Kansas State College. In the spring of this year he visited England to arrange for the publication of his poems.

Claude McKay is a pure blooded Negro, and though we have recently been made aware of some of the more remarkable achievements of African Art typified by the sculpture from Benin, and in music by the Spirituals, this is the first instance of success in poetry with which we in Europe at any rate have been brought into contact. The reasons for this late development are not far to seek, and the difficulties presented by modern literary English as an acquired medium would be sufficient to account for the lacuna ; but the poems here selected may, in the opinion of not a few who have seen them in periodical form, claim a place beside the best work that the present generation is producing in this country.

I.A. RICHARDS

Cambridge, England
September, 1920

Spring in New Hampshire

Too green the springing April grass,
    Too blue the silver-speckled sky,
For me to linger here, alas,
    While happy winds go laughing by,
Wasting the golden hours indoors,
Washing windows and scrubbing floors.

Too wonderful the April night,
    Too faintly sweet the first May flowers,
The stars too gloriously bright,
    For me to spend the evening hours,
When fields are fresh and streams are leaping,
Wearied, exhausted, dully sleeping.

The Spanish Needle

Lovely dainty Spanish needle
    With your yellow flower and white,
Dew bedecked and softly sleeping,
    Do you think of me tonight?

Shadowed by the spreading mango,
    Nodding o'er the rippling stream,
Tell me, dear plant of my childhood,
    Do you of the exile dream?

Do you see me by the brook's side
    Catching crayfish 'neath the stone,
As you did the day you whispered:
    Leave the harmless dears alone?

Do you see me in the meadow
    Coming from the woodland spring
With a bamboo on my shoulder
    And a pail slung from a string?

Do you see me all expectant
    Lying in an orange grove,
While the swee-swees sing above me,
    Waiting for my elf-eyed love?

Lovely dainty Spanish needle,
    Source to me of sweet delight,
In your far-off sunny southland
    Do you dream of me tonight?

The Lynching

His spirit in smoke ascended to high heaven.
His father, by the cruellest way of pain,
Had bidden him to his bosom once again:
The awful sin remained still unforgiven.
All night a bright and solitary star
(Perchance the one that ever guided him,
Yet gave him up at last to Fate's wild whim)
Hung pitifully o'er the swinging char.
Day dawned, and soon the mixed crowds came to view
The ghastly body swaying in the sun:
The women thronged to look, but never a one
Showed sorrow in her eyes of steely blue;
And little lads, lynchers that were to be,
Danced round the dreadful thing in fiendish glee.

To O.E.A.

Your voice is the colour of a robin's breast,
    And there's a sweet sob in it like rain—still rain in the night.
Among the leaves of the trumpet-tree, close to his nesl,
    The pea-dove sings, and each note thrills me with strange delight
Like the words, wet with music, that well from your trembling throat.
    I'm afraid of your eyes, they're so bold,
    Searching me through, reading my thoughts, shining like gold.
But sometimes they are gentle and soft like the dew on the lips of the
        eucharis
Before the sun comes warm with his lover's kiss,
    You are sea-foam, pure with the star's loveliness,
Not mortal, a flower, a fairy, too fair for the beauty-shorn earth,
All wonderful things, all beautiful things, gave of their wealth to your
        birth:
    O I love you so much, not recking of passion, that I feel it is wrong,
    But men will love you, flower, fairy, non-mortal spirit burdened
        with flesh,
    Forever, life-long.

Alfonso, Dressing to Wait at Table, Sings

Alfonso is a handsome bronze-hued lad
    Of subtly-changing and surprising parts;
His moods are storms that frighten and make glad,
    His eyes were made to capture women's hearts.

Down in the glory-hole Alfonso sings
    An olden song of wine and clinking glasses
And riotous rakes; magnificently flings
    Gay kisses to imaginary lasses.

Alfonso's voice of mellow music thrills
    Our swaying forms and steals our hearts with joy;
And, when he soars, his fine falsetto trills
    Are rarest notes of gold without alloy.

But O! Alfonso, wherefore do you sing
    Dream-songs of carefree men and ancient places?
Soon shall we be beset by clamouring
    Of hungry and importunate palefaces.

Flowers of Passion

The dancers have departed, dear,
    And the last song has been sung;
The red-stained glasses mock my gaze
    And the fiddle lies unstrung.

And I'm alone, alone once more,
    Save for your sweet brown face
That comes reproachfully to me
    In this unholy place.

I've kissed a thousand flowers, my own,
    Gone drunk with their perfume;
But found out, when the madness passed,
    You were the one pure bloom.

I've come to realise at last
    How awful it may be
To cut adrift from sacred ties
    And be completely free.

But life grows many flowers, my love,
    Within its garden wall,
And passion's are the strangest
    And the deadliest of all.

To Work

The Dawn! the Dawn, the crimson-tinted comes
Out of the low still skies, over the hills,
New York's fantastic spires and cheerless domes,—
The Dawn! my spirit to its spirit thrills.
Almost the mighty city is asleep,
No pushing crowd, no tramping, tramping feet;
But here and there a few cars, groaning, creep
Along, above and underneath the street,
Bearing their strangely-ghostly burdens by,—
The women and the men of garish nights,
Their eyes wine-weakened and their clothes awry,
Nodding under the strong electric lights.
On through the waning shadows of New York,
Before the Dawn, I wend my way to work.

Morning Joy

At night the wide and level stretch of wold,
Which at high noon had basked in quiet gold,
Far as the eye could see was ghostly white;
Dark was the night save for the snow's weird light.

I drew the shades far down, crept into bed;
Hearing the cold wind moaning overhead
Through the sad pines, my soul, catching its pain,
Went sorrowing with it across the plain.

At dawn behold! the pall of night was gone
Save where a few shrubs melancholy, lone,
Detained part of its shadow. Golden-lipped
The laughing grasses heaven's sweet wine sipped.

The sun rose smiling o'er the river's breast,
And my soul, by his happy spirit blest,
Soared like a bird to greet him in the sky
And drew out of his heart Eternity.

Reminiscences

When the day is at its dimmest
    And the air is wild with snow,
And the city's at its grimmest
    In mine eyes there is a glow . . .
When the day is at its brightest
    And the city is a dream,
And my heart is at its lightest,
    In mine eyes there is a gleam;
For I'm thinking, O I'm thinking,
    Of an old worn sugar-mill
Where the southern sun is sinking—
    Gold and crimson—o'er the hill;
And I hear the toilers talking
    As they shoulder pick and hoe,
And I watch their steady walking
    To the quiet plain below.
O! I see the white stream dashing
    Gay and reckless through the brake,
O'er the root-entwined rocks washing
    Swiftly, madly to the lake;
O! I hear the waters falling,
    Flowing, falling, flowing free,
And the sound of voices calling
    O'er the billows of the sea.

On Broadway

About me young and careless feet
Linger along— the garish street;
   Above, a hundred shouting signs
Shed down their bright fantastic glow
   Upon the merry crowd and lines
Of moving carriages below:
O wonderful is Broadway—only
My heart, my heart is lonely.

Desire naked, linked with Passion,
Goes strutting by in brazen fashion;
   From playhouse, cabaret and inn
The rainbow lights of Broadway blaze
   All gay without, all glad within;
As in a dream I stand and gaze
At Broadway, shining Broadway—only
My heart, my heart is lonely.

Love Song

Heart of the saffron rose,
 Lines of the lily red,
Gold of the buttercup,
 Dew of the daisies' bed,
Flight of the rising bird
 Luring me to the skies,
Smile of an evening star
 Playing before mine eyes,

Rime of the silver morn
 Fair on the green of trees,
Scent of the coffee blooms
 Waking the drowsy bees;
Charming and beautiful,
 Rare are these sights to see;
But more than all and more
 Is your fond heart to me.

NORTH AND SOUTH

O sweet are tropic lands for waking dreams!
 There time and life move lazily along;
There by the banks of blue-and-silver streams
 Grass-sheltered crickets chirp incessant song,
Gay-coloured lizards loll all through the day,
 Their tongues outstretched for careless little flies,
And swarthy children in the fields at play
 Look upward laughing at the smiling skies.
A breath of idleness is in the air
 That casts a subtle spell upon all things,
And love and mating-time are everywhere
 And wonder to life's commonplaces clings.
The fluttering humming-bird darts through the trees
 And dips his long beak in the big bell-flowers,
The leisured buzzard floats upon the breeze
 Riding a crescent cloud for endless hours;
The sea beats softly on the emerald strands,—
O sweet for dainty dreams are tropic lands!

Rest in Peace

No more for you the city's thorny ways,
    The ugly corners of the Negro belt;
The miseries and pains of these harsh days
    By you will never, never again be felt.

No more, if still you wander, will you meet
    With nights of unabating bitterness,
They cannot reach you in your safe retreat,
    The city's hate, the city's prejudice!

'Twas sudden—but your menial task is done,
    The dawn now breaks on you, the dark is over,
The sea is crossed, the longed-for port is won,
    Farewell, oh fare you well! fond friend and lover.

A Memory of June

When June comes dancing o'er the death of May,
    With scarlet roses tinting— her green breast,
And mating thrushes ushering in her day,
    And Earth on tiptoe for her golden guest,

I always see the evening when we met—
    The first of June baptised in tender rain—
And walked home through the wide streets, gleaming wet,
    Arms locked, our warm flesh pulsing with love's pain.

I always see the cheerful little room,
    And in the corner, fresh and white, the bed
Sweet scented with a delicate perfume,
    Wherein for one night only we were wed:

Where in the starlit stillness we lay mute
    And heard the whispering showers all night long,
And your brown burning body was a lute
    Whereon wild passion played his fevered song.

When June comes dancing o'er the death of May,
    With scarlet roses staining her fair feet,
My soul takes leave of me to sing all day
    A night of rare love, perfect and complete.

To Winter

Stay, season of calm love and soulful snows!
There is a subtle sweetness in the sun,
The ripples on the stream's breast gaily run,
The wind more boisterously by me blows,
And each succeeding day now longer grows.
The birds a gladder music have begun,
The squirrel, full of mischief and of fun,
From maples' topmost branch small brown twigs throws.
I read these pregnant signs, know what they mean:
I know that thou art making ready to go.
Oh stay! . . . I fled a land where fields are green
Always, and palms wave gently to and fro,
And winds are balmy, blue brooks ever sheen,
To ease my heart of its impassioned woe.

Winter in the Country

Sweet life! how lovely to be here
    And feel the soft sea-laden breeze
Strike my flushed face, the spruce's fair
    Free limbs to see, the lesser trees'

Bare hands to touch, the sparrow's cheep
    To heed, and watch his nimble flight
Above the short brown grass asleep.
    Love glorious in his friendly might,

Music that every heart could bless,
    And thoughts of life serene, divine,
Beyond my power to express
    Crowd round this lifted heart of mine!

But oh! to leave this paradise
    For the city's dirty basement room,
Where, beauty hidden from the eyes,
    A table, bed, bureau and broom

In corner set, two crippled chairs
    All covered up with dust and grim
With hideousness and scars of years,
    And gaslight burning weird and dim,

Will welcome me . . . And yet, and yet
    The sea-wind here, the winter birds,
The glory of the soft sunset,
    There come to me in words.

After the Winter

Some day, when trees have shed their leaves
    And against the morning's white
The shivering birds beneath the eaves
    Have sheltered for the night,
We'll turn our faces southward, love,
    Toward the summer isle
Where bamboos spire to shafted grove
    And wide-mouthed orchids smile.

And we will seek the quiet hill
    Where towers the cotton tree,
And leaps the laughing crystal rill
    And works the droning bee,
And we will build a cottage there
    Beside an open glade,
With black-ribbed blue-bells blowing near
    And ferns that never fade.

The Tropics in New York

Bananas ripe and green and ginger-root,
    Cocoa in pods and alligator pears,
And tangerines and mangoes and grape fruit,
    Fit for the highest prize at parish fairs,

Set in the window, bringing memories
    Of fruit trees laden by low-singing rills,
And dewy dawns and mystical blue skies
    In benediction over nun-like hills.

Mine eyes grew dim and I could no more gaze,
    A wave of longing through my body swept,
And, hungry for the old, familiar ways,
    I turned aside and bowed my head and wept.

I Shall Return

I shall return again; I shall return
To laugh and love and watch with wonder-eyes,
At golden noon the forest fires burn,
Wafting their blue-black smoke to sapphire skies.
I shall return to loiter by the streams
That bathe the brown blades of the bending grasses,
And realise once more my thousand dreams
Of waters rushing down the mountain passes.
I shall return, to hear the fiddle and fife
Of village dances, dear delicious tunes
That stir the hidden depths of native life,
Stray melodies of dim remembered runes:
I shall return, I shall return again
To ease my mind of long, long years of pain.

THE CASTAWAYS

The vivid grass with visible delight
Springing triumphant from the pregnant earth;
And butterflies, and sparrows in brief flight
Chirping and dancing for the season's birth,
And dandelions and rare daffodils
That hold the deep-stirred heart with hands of gold
And thrushes sending forth their joyous trills;
Not these, not these did I at first behold:
But seated on the benches daubed with green,
The castaways of earth, some fast asleep,
With many a withered woman wedged between,
And over all life's shadows dark and deep:
Moaning I turned away, for misery
I have the strength to bear but not to see.

December 1919

Last night I heard your voice, mother,
 The words you sang to me
When I, a little barefoot boy,
 Knelt down against your knee.

And tears gushed from my heart, mother,
 And passed beyond its wall,
But though the fountain reached my throat
 The drops refused to fall.

'Tis ten years since you died, mother,
 Just ten dark years of pain,
And oh, I only wish that I
 Could weep for once again.

FLAME-HEART

So much have I forgotten in ten years,
    So much in ten brief years; I have forgot
What time the purple apples come to juice
    And what month brings the shy forget-me-not;
Forgotten is the special, startling season
    Of some beloved tree's flowering and fruiting,
What time of year the ground doves brown the fields
    And fill the noonday with their curious fluting:
I have forgotten much, but still remember
The poinscttia's red, blood-red in warm December.

I still recall the honey-fever grass,
    But I cannot bring back to mind just when
We rooted them out of the ping-wing path
    To stop the mad bees in the rabbit pen.
I often try to think in what sweet month
    The languid painted ladies used to dapple
The yellow bye road mazing from the main,
    Sweet with the golden threads of the rose-apple:
I have forgotten, strange, but quite remember
The poinsettia's red, blood-red in warm December.

What weeks, what months, what time o'the mild year
    We cheated school to have our fling at tops?
What days our wine-thrilled bodies pulsed with joy
    Feasting upon blackberries in the copse?
Oh some I know! I have embalmed the days,
    Even the sacred moments, when we played,
All innocent of passion uncorrupt,
    At noon and evening in the flame-heart's shade:
We were so happy, happy,—I remember
Beneath the poinsettia's red in warm December.

In Bondage

I would be wandering in distant fields
Where man, and bird, and beast, lives leisurely,
And the old earth is kind and ever yields
Her goodly gifts to all her children free;
Where life is fairer, lighter, less demanding,
And boys and girls have time and space for play
Before they come to years of understanding,—
Somewhere I would be singing, far away;
For life is greater than the thousand wars
Men wage for it in their insatiate lust,
And will remain like the eternal stars
When all that is today is ashes and dust:
But I am bound with you in your mean graves,
Oh black men, simple slaves of ruthless slaves.

Harlem Shadows

I hear the halting footsteps of a lass
    In Negro Harlem when the night lets fall
Its veil. I see the shapes of girls who pass
    Eager to heed desire's insistent call:
Ah, little dark girls, who in slippered feet
Go prowling throught the night from street to street.

Through the long night until the silver break
    Of day the little gray feet know no rest,
Through the lone night until the last snow-flake
    Has dropped from heaven upon the earth's white breast,
The dusky, half-clad girls of tired feet
Are trudging, thinly shod, from street to street.

Ah, stern harsh world, that in the wretched way
    Of poverty, dishonour and disgrace,
Has pushed the timid little feet of clay.
    The sacred brown feet of my fallen race!
Ah, heart of me, the weary, weary feet
In Harlem wandering from street to street.

The Harlem Dancer

Applauding youths laughed with young prostitutes
And watched her perfect, half-clothed body sway;
Her voice was like the sound of blended flutes
Blown by black players upon a picnic day.
She sang and danced on gracefully and calm,
The light gauze hanging loose about her form;
To me she seemed a proudly-swaying palm
Grown lovelier for passing through a storm.
Upon her swarthy neck black, shiny curls
Profusely fell; and, tossing coins in praise,
The wine-flushed, bold-eyed boys, and even the girls,
Devoured her with eager, passionate gaze:
But, looking at her falsely-smiling face,
I knew her self was not in that strange place.

A PRAYER

(For Max Eastman)

'Mid the discordant noises of the day I hear thee calling,
I stumble as I fare along Earth's way; keep me from falling.

Mine eyes are open but they cannot see for gloom of night;
I can no more than lift my heart to thee for inward light.

The wild and fiery passion of my youth consumes my soul;
In agony I turn to thee for truth and self control.

For Passion and all the pleasures it can give will die the death;
But this of me eternally must live, thy borrowed breath.

'Mid the discordant noises of the day I hear thee calling,
I stumble as I fare along Earth's way; keep me from falling.

The Barrier

I must not gaze at them although
    Your eyes are dawning day;
I must not watch you as you go
    Your sun-illumined way;

I hear but I must never heed
    The fascinating note,
Which, fluting like a river reed,
    Comes from your trembling throat;

I must not see upon your face
    Love's softly glowing spark;
For there's the barrier of race,
    You're fair and I am dark.

When Dawn Comes to the City

The tired cars go grumbling by,
    The moaning, groaning cars,
And the old milk carts go rumbling by
    Under the same dull stars.
Out of the tenements, cold as stone,
    Dark figures start for work;
I watch them sadly shuffle on,
    'Tis dawn, dawn in New York.

But I would be on the island of the sea,
    In the heart of the island of the sea,
Where the cocks are crowing, crowing, crowing,
    And the hens are cackling in the rose-apple tree,
Where the old draft-horse is neighing, neighing, neighing
    Out on the brown dew-silvered lawn,
    And the tethered cow is lowing, lowing, lowing,
And dear old Ned is braying, braying, braying,
And the shaggy Nannie goat is calling, calling, calling
    From her little trampled corner of the long wide lea
That stretches to the waters of the hill-stream falling
    Sheer upon the flat rocks joyously!
    There, oh there! on the island of the sea
        There I would be at dawn.

The tired cars go grumbling by,
    The crazy, lazy cars,
And the same milk-carts go rumbling by
    Under the dying stars.
A lonely newsboy hurries by,
    Humming a recent ditty;
Red streaks strike through the gray of the sky,
    The dawn comes to the city.

But I would be on the island of the sea,
In the heart of the island of the sea,

Where the cocks are crowing, crowing, crowing,
And the hens are cackling in the rose-apple tree,
Where the old draft-horse is neighing, neighing, neighing
Out on the brown dew-silvered lawn,
And the tethered cow is lowing, lowing, lowing,
And dear old Ned is braying, braying, braying,
And the shaggy Nannie goat is calling, calling, calling
From her little trampled corner of the long wide lea
That stretches to the waters of the hill-stream falling
Sheer upon the flat rocks joyously!
There, oh there! on the island of the sea
There I would be at dawn.

The Choice

O you would clothe me in silken frocks
    And house me from the cold,
And bind with bright bands my glossy locks
    And buy me chains of gold;

And give me—meekly to do my will—
    The hapless sons of men:—
But the wild goat bounding on the barren hill
    Droops in the grassy pen.

Sukee River

Thou sweet-voiced stream that first gavest me drink,
    Watched o'er me when I floated on thy breast,
What black-faced boy now gambols on thy brink,
    Or finds beneath thy rocks a place of rest?
What naked lad doth linger long by thee,
    And run and tumble in the sun-scorched sand,
Or heed the pea-dove in the wild fig tree,
    While I am roaming in an alien land?
No wonder that my heart is happy never,
I have been faithless to thee, Sukee River.

When from my early wandering I returned,
    Did I not promise to remain for aye?
Yet instantly for other regions yearned
    And wearied of thee in a single day.
Thy murmurs sound now in my anguished ears,
    Creating in my heart a world of pain;
I see thee wistful flowing down the years
    And though I pine, afar I must remain:
No wonder that my feet are faltering ever,
I have been faithless to thee, Sukee River.

Though other boys may frolic by thy side,
    I know their merry moods thou dost not heed
When I, O mother of my soul and bride,
    Lie on strange breasts and on strange kisses feed.
Sometimes, kind fate permitting me, I dream
    I am floating on thy bosom of deep blue,
A child again, beloved, unchanging stream;
    But soon I wake to find it all untrue:
I vowed that never, never would we sever,
But I've been faithless to thee, Sukee River.

Exhortation

Through the pregnant universe rumbles life's terrific thunder
   And Earth's bowels quake with terror; strange and terrible storms
      break,
Lightning-torches flame the heavens, kindling souls of men
      thereunder:
   Africa! long ages sleeping, Oh my motherland, awake!

In the East the clouds glow crimson with the new dawn that is
      breaking,
   And its golden glory fills the western skies:—
   Oh my brothers and my sisters, wake! arise!
For the new birth rends the old earth and the very dead are waking,
   Ghosts are turned flesh, throwing off the grave's disguise,
   And the foolish, even children, are made wise;
For the big earth groans in travail for the strong, new world in
      making—
   Oh my brothers, dreaming for dim centuries,
   Wake from sleeping; to the East turn, turn you eyes!

Oh the night is sweet for sleeping, but the shining day's for working;
   Sons of the seductive night, for your children's children's sake,
From the deep primeval forests where the crouching leopard's lurking,
   Lift your heavy-lidded eyes,—Ethiopia! awake!

In the East the clouds glow crimson with the new dawn that is
      breaking,
   And its golden glory fills the western skies:—
   Oh my brothers and my sisters, wake! arise!
For the new birth rends the old earth and the very dead are waking,
   Ghosts are turned flesh, throwing off the grave's disguise,
   And the foolish, even children, are made wise;
For the big earth groans in travail for the strong, new world in
      making—
   Oh my brothers, dreaming for long centuries,
   Wake from sleeping; to the East turn, turn your eyes!

                                                       CLAUDE MCKAY

A Note About the Author

Claude McKay (1889–1948) was a Jamaican poet and novelist. Born in Sunny Ville, Jamaica, McKay was raised in a strict Baptist family alongside seven siblings. Sent to live with his brother Theo, a journalist, at the age of nine, McKay excelled in school while reading poetry in his free time. In 1912, he published his debut collection *Songs of Jamaica*, the first poems written in Jamaican Patois to appear in print. That same year, he moved to the United States to attend the Tuskegee Institute, though he eventually transferred to Kansas State University. Upon his arrival in the South, he was shocked by the racism and segregation experienced by Black Americans, which—combined with his reading of W. E. B. Du Bois' work—inspired him to write political poems and to explore the principles of socialism. He moved to New York in 1914 without completing his degree, turning his efforts to publishing poems in *The Seven Arts* and later *The Liberator*, where he would serve as co-executive editor from 1919 to 1922. Over the next decade, he would devote himself to communism and Black radicalism, joining the Industrial Workers of the World, opposing the efforts of Marcus Garvey and the NAACP, and travelling to Britain and Russia to meet with communists and write articles for various leftist publications. McKay, a bisexual man, was also a major figure of the Harlem Renaissance, penning *Harlem Shadows* (1922), a successful collection of poems, and *Home to Harlem* (1928), an award-winning novel exploring Harlem's legendary nightlife.

A Note from the Publisher

Spanning many genres, from non-fiction essays to literature classics to children's books and lyric poetry, Mint Edition books showcase the master works of our time in a modern new package. The text is freshly typeset, is clean and easy to read, and features a new note about the author in each volume. Many books also include exclusive new introductory material. Every book boasts a striking new cover, which makes it as appropriate for collecting as it is for gift giving. Mint Edition books are only printed when a reader orders them, so natural resources are not wasted. We're proud that our books are never manufactured in excess and exist only in the exact quantity they need to be read and enjoyed.

Discover more of your favorite classics with Bookfinity™.

- Track your reading with custom book lists.
- Get great book recommendations for your personalized Reader Type.
- Add reviews for your favorite books.
- AND MUCH MORE!

Visit **bookfinity.com** and take the fun Reader Type quiz to get started.

Enjoy our classic and modern companion pairings!

9 781513 299907